THE THINGS I SEE
A collection of short, witty, satirical poems

F.OMOSOLA

All rights reserved. No part of this publication may be reproduced, distributed, or transmitted in any form or by any means, including photocopying, recording, or other electronic or mechanical methods, without the prior written permission of the publisher, except in the case of brief quotations embodied in critical reviews and certain other non-commercial uses permitted by copyright law.

FORTUNE OMOSOLA © 2024

ISBN (Paperback) - 978-1-917267-22-9

ISBN (E-Book) - 978-1-917267-23-6

Published by Nubian Republic on behalf of Palmwine Publishing Limited Nigeria

Email: info@palmwinepublishing.com

Address- UK: 86-90, Paul Street, London EC2A 4NE

Address-Nigeria: 1A Jos Road Bukuru, Plateau State, Nigeria.

www.palmwinepublishing.com
www.raffiapress.com
www.nuciferaanalysis.com

A QUIET ENTRY

'When a woman gets tired of her husband, she kills him so she can live forever...'

'Elegance fraternizes with the eye, so does the ambush of deception...'

'Read all you can while you can; find all you can read and master it because life itself is all in a page less book...'

– **F.Omosola**

Table of Contents

A Quiet Entry	3
Dedication	6
Preface	7
Lust	9
Behind The Scene	10
Blunted Knives	11
Trotter	13
Labbadia	14
Dead Ends Are Not Ruins	15
The Things I See	17
Disruptive	19
Plastics Don't Die	20
Your Version of Truth is Familiar	21
Two	22
The Piety of Suffering	23

Impassioned	25
Stained Lillies	27
Mai Mahiu	29
Adunni	30
The Hymn of Shame	31
Alive	33
Nuclear	34
Lovelorn	35
Football	36
Interregnum	37
Nothing is Dangerous	39
Pain	40
You Are Not Ready	42
Chaos	43

Dedication

To my angels, **Dolabomi, Mofeohunoluwase** and the one to come this is for you and your mother, **Adunni.**

I have pieced together many among these from native intelligence and plentiful observations of all human entries however small.

We would cross the oceans together to see the human planet, just believe.

Preface

"The destiny of earth is to endure." — **Kofi Awoonor**

Life's path is rarely straight. It twists through moments of beauty, pain, resilience, and hope. In this collection, *The Things I See*, Fortune Omosola opens a window into the raw and vivid experiences that shape our world. Through the cadence of his verses, he paints a portrait of modern existence—our joys, our sorrows, and the unyielding human spirit that perseveres.

As a broadcast journalist, spoken word artist, and poet, Omosola has mastered the art of observation. This collection, his third volume following _Labyrinth_ and _Bold is Your Fate_, brings together his keen insights into life's deepest realities. From the silent suffering of the marginalized to the vibrant rhythm of Nigerian nightclubs, his words capture a world in flux, marked by both chaos and calm.

Omosola's passion extends beyond poetry. His voice resonates across multiple mediums, whether through his four published books, or through his platform, _**Jollofmash**_, where he addresses vital issues like climate change, public health, and art. Here, in *The Things I See*, the spoken word finds its written form, creating a symphony of thought and feeling, a dialogue with the human condition.

This collection invites readers to pause, reflect, and see the world anew through the eyes of a poet who embraces both the ordinary and the extraordinary. The journey through these pages is one of discovery, both of the world around us and the one within.

- **DR. ENEYO GEOFREY**

LUST

When the demon called lust takes charge

There are no holds,

An ugly chicken throws you out of the driver's seat

Pffft-

___Into a small cage

Where your fate comes in flashes:

A butt, a derriere, a rock hard load of mouthful veins;

Bouts of perennial jabbing against a woman's private appeal -

This thing winks at your soul and riles you over,

Till you break into a conversational alarm system,

Your purity ebbs away.

The driver speeds off with your life,

Leaves you tied at the exhaust

Inhaling the fumes of emptiness,

Then it fades into the unseen distance.

BEHIND THE SCENE

A quiet voice behind the microphone must resonate with power—

Come fully formed, loved, and efficient.

It is the eyes for blind men,

The soul for the bereaved,

Thoughts for the kind,

Every pressing,

To heal and burn.

It is not for the inchoate,

Nor for those trudging under searchlights.

BLUNTED KNIVES

You'll think Nigerians are poor until you see them in nightclubs—swallowing decibels.

They stack bottles on the derrieres of Jezebels, chanting ad hominems.

In the crush of morning, they drift on complaints, curse the devil,

Crying till their teeth fall from their mouths.

They sit in churches, seething;

In fast food joints, grinning—

Plunder parties with Naira notes

Float on newspapers like ghosts.

They hum.

They dance, crawl,

Blame,

Howl,

Sink peerless into the infinite abyss of social media...
to deride

Till the wasteland perishes.

TROTTER

I will trot around the world

Before I see it in a blink.

Solvents? No.

It's hard before it sinks.

I come whole,

Fast.

Save me before it lasts—

Emotions through empty bottles,

Sleep it through in cars.

LABBADIA

Nigeria's answer to zilch.

He is the German that reverses insanity

Before it starts,

The rainmaker that lives in the desert.

DEAD ENDS ARE NOT RUINS

Nigeria was Eden before heaven left it in the hands of recidivists—

To plough and plunder;

It was captured complete and laid in the mouths of lions who couldn't swallow it.

Ailing in an insatiable state,

Drenched, famished, hanging—

A coup de grâce failing to come.

Honour the king? Who?

The one who rides on the chariots of corruption?

Who?

The one who flies the flag of fear?

Who?

The one who chases out tongues with spears?

Who?

The one whose broth tastes like blood?

THE THINGS I SEE

The pocket has a story

No matter how deep

It brings families together

Fathom wars and disciples men

Money, isn't it?

A craving yelling at my factotum

Outside my body, is me

The one caught looking at the oval stable

Reaching for heights far above his head

Stoic,

Just aware that patterns may change

If the metaphysical aligns with such primordial prospects

If,

Only my mind could meditate beyond this maniac pleasure

That I wouldn't let consume my soul

But what about the routine?

The routine of giving birth, working, fighting, hiding, praying, hoping, dying-

The things I see are unearthly.

DISRUPTIVE

Old roads lead to hell,

New ones are for upstarts.

Tragedy lives in a burning quiet

As the world winds around a needle.

Of what use is masochism?

PLASTICS DON'T DIE

They live on,

Indulging the toxicity of humans

Through their immortal manifold.

Transfixing earth under their bulk,

From plant to monster.

YOUR VERSION OF TRUTH IS FAMILIAR

You don't know the truth until it wins you over,

Then slowly tears you apart.

It makes you shudder when you're alone

But face the crowd, untangled.

You would crow,

Howl, hiss, retreat.

It's a winning soldier bearing crucibles all by itself till the war cements.

TWO

Two little ducks in a pond,

Tossed in circles by unholy vibration,

Letting go of uncertainty,

Floating on water without end.

THE PIETY OF SUFFERING

Some say the best way to die is to see the world end.

A man retreats into a hospice and smiles.

Checkmate!

If the poor man is angry or wounded, this axiom would serve:

He has had enough, end it!

Same for slaves in modern apparel and fat bank accounts drowning.

"Easy," says the rich man with a stick and flame,

Walking befuddled, hand in beard,

Never having enough,

Leaving empty.

Suffering—it's all of it,

All in it.

Who else? The power broker?

Hitler?

Democracy bloggers licking derision, or religion panicking in fate?

What purpose will humanity serve when earth closes its shop?

IMPASSIONED

Motherland, hand me with care.

Your paws are pressing my neck.

When it rains, it pours.

The flood is entering by legs;

My jaws are hurting.

Let me breathe.

Cover me with your robes,

Let me heal.

Your words are farting.

Hardly was I told about this farming.

I see the old men stay silent,

Their faces tell me many things.

My heart has emigrated like the rest of us into untold places

Where war and second class meet.

I see the world from here

In the fullness of a small measure,

My eyes clawing through its cloying

Before men and their menace are transfigured.

It's all too familiar until the puppeteers start translating.

STAINED LILLIES

Aren't we all Luddites before we came here?

Our shoulders bleeding from pompous,

Our heads stuck in what knowledge begot.

Hillbillies sauntering in coloured castles—

Aren't we the stained lilies on the field?

The ones with timeless ornaments drizzled before a slaughter?

Let's not carry this poison to sleep—

The craze of numbers hording our dreams...

In all of modernity, I have found nothing more than a pen

To scribble out speleologists in their farthest

Praying for the courage to see through the darkness,

Holding on to the cliff when it's hardest.

Measuring nature against its harm,

At home is a pound of flesh.

MAI MAHIU

When rain falls in Mahiu,

It raises stones and hurls them at houses

As if insulted by the humans that walk across it.

Strangers are beckoned to the bottom of the bed

As the wind and storm burst into a song.

After a seedy copulation, there is an ejaculation of flood and damage,

The riddles of mankind taken with it.

At dusk, men sprawl on their wives in the pool of their own poverty.

ADUNNI

Rolling back years of African fiddle,

The aplomb of black and white where it fits.

Herself an adulation of the rainbow when it spurns after rain,

Her face the golden brown of desert heat.

THE HYMN OF SHAME

There is nothing here that you haven't seen before:

The eyes of children garnished with hunger,

Firmer hands lounging later on their carcasses,

Middlemen shaking hands with vultures inside their rampart,

An army of slaves led by a blind few—

Your retina must be worn out by now.

When the speech abides by the table and guns sing in the field,

Do we lay still on our turgid belly or hum the hymn of shame?

There is nothing your ears haven't heard before:

Lies that buzz on free food,

The anarchy of worms,

An old woman singing fables.

The coast won't clear by noon.

ALIVE

When darkness crumble at dawn

The energy of light floods the heart of men

To take control,

To rewrite dreams

To steam beyond the empty pages of fear.

NUCLEAR

The sky falling is not blue

It is pale with misfortune

Harvesting itself through the flaws of man-made rockets

Beating down the agony of thunder,

Who are these men, who merry at their creation?

The gloss of the Milky Way is burning

Drawn to it is the borderline –

An eternal damnation not approved by the ancient finger.

LOVELORN

There is nothing to miss when the heart is empty,

Vacuous, shaved, bereaved, un-placated by the fever of *feeling*

It thereafter dangles in a void

The wild beats of sorrow drowns it

The heart then asks its owner, where have you been?

No response.

The head spins like a dart in fury towards the bull eye of regret.

FOOTBALL

Legs hurry after it,

A round piece of leather

Transformed through trickery

Its patches feinted from left to right,

Sliding on grass, sand over the air

Embracing the unending paint of emotions

There is pain, there is laughter

It is the life men live before this round thing melts into the net.

INTERREGNUM

Who will be the next president

A suave, a bot, a bum,

No, a mouse,

Ruckus...

The trick of it works better with the *light-handed*

The cookie jar is jarring

It is now that the tongues must stick

I say who?

A soloist, a moron?

God forbid! These normads are sadists

Took us back 30 years through the desert of their minds,

We wont have them,

But on whose order?

These young seniles?

Save your breath! Hold it!!

Nothing but tactical hypocrisy!!

Answer my question comrade in palms!

I say who?

Nobody,

Sir.

NOTHING IS DANGEROUS

The danger of nothing

Is in the doing,

Not moving, barren

A stagnation folding on rue

The zero attitude of retentive calmness

Slapping the orbit that is hardly unkind

If those who dig can sell,

Of what use is the banana garden?

PAIN

What do I call these people who have no memory of their pain,

Loveless or endangered?

This preponderance of ignorance cannot continue,

What is the ultimate gain?

Genocide or greed?

With what aim do their minds shoot,

-From a colourless vision

Why are they so bolshie?

Who will quench the fire engraving,

Or unchain the spirits held by squirts of blood

Defiant must be their graves_

Someone should be livid! -

Angry at this sovereign rupture

The withered hands can't build utopia

There is none bold enough to demand

Answers from these sit-tights!

YOU ARE NOT READY

The fallen angels are in flight

Armed with the cudgel of darkness

Can't you see?

-Your soul is fighting for light – barely,

And they detest it

While the ghosts of avarice and lechery

Build

Mercenaries in men

A legion

The ones who lay golden bricks on the –curse

Bob's Khan invention.

When the moon relishes blood

Sun to the unknow,

Will you embrace the differnet versions of blood?

CHAOS

When you laugh

Remember Nigeria

-hide your cackling in the putrid,

Smell of its algophilia.

If you cry, don't spill over yet,

Let your tears paint a hue,

When the chicken has its feathers intact

It won't hurry to imitate th duck

When innocent blood

Roams indignant

The living will suffer.

Oh

Since the quislings have set peace on fire

Should we all retire to bear the anguish

Or stand back to douse the flames?

This house has fallen,

The debris – dessicated.

About the Author

**Fortune Omosola** is an experienced broadcast journalist, content creator, Voice actor, spoken word artist, and published poet with a passion for unorthodox storytelling that transcends mediums. A seasoned news content professional and voice artist, he brings a depth of insight and emotion to both his written and spoken word. With four published books on Amazon, including his latest collection, _The Things I See_, Omosola continues to captivate audiences with his unique voice.

Beyond his career in journalism, Fortune is a devoted family man, sharing his life with his wife and two lovely daughters. His work is deeply influenced by his personal experiences and his commitment to shedding light on the pressing issues of our time, from climate change to public health. His popular online platform, www.Jollofmash.com.ng, further amplifies his engagement with topics that shape our world, weaving art, news events, and activism into a compelling narrative.

Fortune Omosola's words resonate with both heart and intellect, making him a voice that speaks to our shared human experience.

www.ingramcontent.com/pod-product-compliance
Lightning Source LLC
Chambersburg PA
CBHW060035180426
43196CB00045B/2692